CREDIT MASTERY

Credit Mastery

Unlocking the Secrets to a Stellar Score

B. VINCENT

QuillQuest Publishers

Contents

Chapter 1: Understanding Credit Scores

Definition and Significance

Understanding what a FICO rating addresses is fundamental in exploring the complicated universe of individual accounting. Basically, a FICO rating is a mathematical portrayal of a singular's reliability, refined from different monetary ways of behaving and exchanges. It fills in as a vital measurement for banks and monetary organizations to survey the gamble related with stretching out credit to a person.

Digging further, a FICO rating isn't only a number; it exemplifies a monetary standing worked over the long haul through mindful getting and reimbursement propensities. Each monetary choice, from charge card use to advance reimbursements, adds to molding this score. Thusly, understanding the meaning of keeping a good FICO rating is critical for anybody looking for monetary soundness and thriving.

A heavenly FICO rating opens ways to a horde of chances. It can mean the contrast between getting a home loan at a good loan fee or confronting over the top getting costs. Besides, property managers, insurance agency, and, surprisingly, potential bosses might investigate financial assessments to measure a singular's unwavering quality and reliability.

Fundamentally, a decent FICO rating isn't simply a number; it is a demonstration of monetary reasonability and obligation. It enables people to get to better monetary items, appreciate lower loan fees, and at last, accomplish their monetary objectives no sweat. Understanding the gravity of this mathematical portrayal establishes the groundwork for dominating one's credit process and opening a universe of monetary potential outcomes.

Factors Influencing Your Score

Unwinding the secret behind your financial assessment includes analyzing the different variables that impact its estimation. These variables act as the structure blocks of your financial soundness, molding a definitive mathematical portrayal that banks examine.

Installment History: At the center of your FICO assessment lies your installment history, mirroring your history of making convenient installments using a loan accounts. Reliably covering bills on time shows unwavering quality and monetary obligation, decidedly affecting your score.

Credit Use: Another vital determinant is your credit use proportion, which estimates how much credit you're utilizing contrasted with your all out accessible credit. Keeping this proportion low, preferably beneath 30%, signals dependable credit the board and can support your score.

Length of Record as a consumer: The time span you've been utilizing credit likewise assumes a huge part. A more extended record gives a more exhaustive image of your monetary propensities and soundness, possibly supporting your score.

Kinds of Credit Records: Variety in the sorts of credit accounts you make due, for example, Mastercards, portion advances, and home loans, can add to a balanced credit profile. Exhibiting dependable administration across various kinds of credit can upgrade your score.

Late Credit Requests: Each time you apply for new credit, a hard request is recorded on your credit report, which can briefly ding your score. Restricting the recurrence of credit requests demonstrates monetary judiciousness and can assist with keeping a sound FICO rating.

Understanding what these elements transaction and mean for your FICO rating is essential in creating a procedure to improve and keep a heavenly credit profile. By proactively dealing with these components, people can apply more noteworthy command over their monetary predetermination and make ready for long haul monetary achievement.

Kinds of Financial assessments

Exploring the scene of FICO ratings includes understanding the different exhibit of scoring models used by banks and monetary establishments. While the credit rating is maybe the most broadly perceived, there exists a large number of other scoring models, each with its own strategy and subtleties.

FICO Score: Created by the Fair Isaac Enterprise, the credit rating stays the highest quality level in credit scoring, used by most of moneylenders in their dynamic cycles. It considers factors, for example, installment history, credit use, length of record, sorts of credit records, and late credit requests to produce a score going from 300 to 850.

VantageScore: Acquainted as a contender with FICO, the VantageScore was created cooperatively by the three significant credit departments: Experian, Equifax, and TransUnion. This scoring model utilizes a comparable scope of 300 to 850 and assesses financial soundness utilizing comparative rules, yet for certain distinctions in weighting and scoring system.

Industry-Explicit Scores: notwithstanding broad financial assessments, certain enterprises use particular scoring models custom fitted to their particular necessities. For example, the car business frequently utilizes auto-explicit scores to survey a singular's probability of reimbursing a car credit, while the home loan industry might use contract explicit scores for home advance endorsements.

Altered Scores: A few loan specialists might foster their restrictive scoring models customized to their one of a kind gamble evaluation rules and client socioeconomics. These re-did scores might consolidate extra data of interest past conventional credit data to refine credit choices further.

Understanding the subtleties and varieties among these different scoring models is fundamental for shoppers trying to decipher their financial assessments really. While the particular score might vary relying upon the model utilized, the basic standards of capable credit the board stay predictable across all scoring procedures. By really getting to know the complexities of credit scoring, people can engage themselves to settle on informed monetary choices and work towards accomplishing a heavenly credit profile.

Significance of a Decent FICO rating

Getting a handle on the significance of keeping a decent FICO rating rises above simple mathematical importance; it epitomizes the embodiment of monetary strengthening and opportunity. A heavenly FICO rating isn't simply a respectable symbol; it is a passage to a universe of monetary potential outcomes and benefits.

Admittance to Good Advance Terms: One of the most unmistakable advantages of a high FICO rating is the capacity to get to credit at positive terms. Moneylenders are more disposed to stretch out advances to people with superb records, offering lower loan fees, higher credit cutoff points, and better reimbursement terms.

Lower Financing costs: A decent FICO assessment means lower loan costs on charge cards, contracts, vehicle advances, and different types of credit. This implies critical investment funds over the existence of a credit, permitting people to keep a greater amount of their well deserved cash and accomplish their monetary objectives all the more effectively.

Higher Acknowledge Cutoff points: People with great FICO ratings frequently appreciate higher credit limits, giving more noteworthy monetary adaptability and buying power. This can be especially advantageous during crises or while making critical buys, managing the cost of people the capacity to explore surprising costs or quickly jump all over chances without unnecessary monetary strain.

Upgraded Monetary Open doors: Past getting, a decent FICO rating opens ways to a plenty of monetary open doors. Landowners might lean toward occupants with great credit while choosing tenants, insurance agency might offer lower charges, and businesses might consider reliability as a figure recruiting choices. Moreover, a solid credit profile can work with endorsement for tenant contracts, utility administrations, and even cell contracts.

At last, a decent FICO rating isn't just about monetary exchanges; it is tied in with building a strong starting point for long haul monetary achievement and security. It reflects capable monetary propensities, judicious navigation, and a promise to financial obligation. By perceiving the significance of keeping a decent FICO rating, people can bridle its ability to accomplish their fantasies and desires, secure in the information that they are laying the preparation for a more brilliant monetary future.

Chapter 2: Building a Strong Credit Foundation

Laying out Record of loan repayment

Setting out on the excursion to fabricate a strong credit establishment is similar to laying the foundation of your monetary future. At the core of this try lies the urgent step of laying out your record — a record of your getting and reimbursement exercises that shapes the bedrock of your financial soundness.

Significance of Opening Your Most memorable Credit Record: For people new to the universe of credit, getting that debut credit account denotes the initiation of their credit process. Whether it's a Mastercard, a got credit, or a store card, this underlying step is essential in launching the most common way of building a record of loan repayment. Without a record as a consumer, loan specialists come up short on vital information to evaluate your gamble level, possibly preventing your capacity to get to credit from now on.

The most effective method to Begin Building Credit Mindfully: While the possibility of overseeing credit might appear to be overwhelming from the get go, finding a way proactive ways to fabricate credit capably lays the basis for a solid monetary future. This involves utilizing credit reasonably, making ideal installments, and trying not to maximize credit limits. By exhibiting mindful getting conduct all along, people can set themselves on a direction toward a vigorous credit profile and open a bunch of monetary open doors.

Generally, laying out your record of loan repayment isn't simply about acquiring admittance to credit — it's tied in with establishing the groundwork for monetary strengthening and autonomy. By moving toward building credit mindfully, people prepare for a long period of reasonable monetary administration and open the way to a universe of monetary conceivable outcomes.

Overseeing Credit Mindfully

Whenever you've made the vital stride of opening your most memorable credit account, the following stage in building areas of strength for an establishment spins around the persevering administration of credit. Overseeing credit capably involves a progression of key activities pointed toward exhibiting monetary discipline and unwavering quality to moneylenders and leasers.

Ways to make On-Time Installments: Ideal installment of acknowledge commitments remains as a foundation of dependable credit the executives. Missing even a solitary installment can unfavorably affect your FICO rating and generally speaking monetary wellbeing. In this way, it's basic to lay out a framework for guaranteeing brief installment of bills, whether through setting up programmed installments or executing suggestions to remain focused.

Keeping Credit Use Low: One more key part of mindful credit the executives includes keeping your credit usage proportion — how much credit you're utilizing contrasted with your absolute accessible credit — low. In a perfect world, this proportion shouldn't surpass 30%, as surpassing this edge can flag monetary pain to moneylenders. By deliberately holding Mastercard adjusts under control and keeping away from over the top spending, people can keep a solid credit usage proportion and reinforce their reliability.

Basically, overseeing credit dependably is tied in with developing restrained monetary propensities and sticking to sound cash the board standards. By making on-time installments and keeping credit use low, people shield their FICO ratings as well as position themselves for more noteworthy monetary open doors later on.

Broadening Your Credit Portfolio

Chasing building areas of strength for an establishment, one of the best procedures includes broadening your credit portfolio. As opposed to depending exclusively on one sort of credit account, broadening involves investigating and overseeing different credit records to exhibit a balanced monetary profile.

Investigating Various Sorts of Credit Records: Credit comes in different structures, each with its exceptional qualities and advantages. From customary charge cards to portion advances and credit extensions, differentiating your credit portfolio includes considering the variety of choices accessible and choosing those that line up with your monetary objectives and conditions. By broadening the kinds of credit accounts you make due, you show to moneylenders your capacity to capably deal with various types of credit, subsequently upgrading your reliability.

Advantages of Overseeing Different Credit Types: Dealing with an assorted exhibit of credit accounts offers a few benefits past just supporting your FICO rating. It can give adaptability in overseeing income, offer admittance to various credit items customized to explicit necessities, and add to a more extensive monetary range of abilities. Besides, various credit the executives can moderate gamble by spreading credit commitments across various records, decreasing dependence on any single wellspring of credit.

Fundamentally, enhancing your credit portfolio is about proactively overseeing risk and advancing monetary open doors. By investigating various sorts of credit accounts and decisively integrating them into your monetary tool compartment, you reinforce your acknowledge establishment as well as position yourself for more noteworthy monetary adaptability and strength even with changing financial conditions.

Observing Your Credit Report

A urgent part of building and keeping major areas of strength for an establishment is the normal observing of your credit report. Your acknowledge report fills in as an extensive record of your record of loan repayment, enumerating your getting and reimbursement exercises, as well as any potential warnings that might affect your financial soundness.

Significance of Normal Check-Ups: Routinely exploring your credit report permits you to remain informed about your monetary standing and personality any inconsistencies or blunders that may incorrectly ponder your reliability. By recognizing and resolving these issues immediately, you can forestall likely harm shockingly score and relieve the gamble of extortion or fraud.

The most effective method to Question Errors: If you find mistakes or disparities on your credit report, it's crucial for make a quick move to correct them. This commonly includes recording a question with the credit department detailing the mistake and giving supporting documentation to prove your case. By following the legitimate debate goal strategies, you can guarantee that your credit report precisely mirrors your record as a consumer and monetary standing.

Basically, checking your credit report is a proactive measure that engages you to protect your reliability and monetary standing. By remaining cautious and tending to any inconsistencies or mistakes expeditiously, you can keep areas of strength for an establishment and open the way to a universe of monetary open doors and security.

Chapter 3: Strategies for Improving Your Credit Score

Taking care of Obligation Decisively

Leaving on the excursion to further develop your FICO rating starts with an essential way to deal with taking care of existing obligation. Obligation, while frequently undeniable, can weigh vigorously on your FICO rating whenever left ignored. Consequently, concocting an arrangement to handle obligation decisively is vital in the mission for a more grounded monetary balance.

Investigate Various Strategies: With regards to taking care of obligation, there are different ways to deal with consider. Two famous techniques are the snowball and torrential slide draws near. The snowball technique includes taking care of obligations from littlest to biggest, paying little heed to loan fees, while the torrential slide strategy centers around handling obligations with the most elevated financing costs first.

Understanding these techniques and picking one that lines up with your monetary objectives and inclinations is the most vital move toward thinking up an obligation reimbursement system that works for you.

Focus on Obligations for Most extreme Effect: Not all obligations are made equivalent, and focusing on them decisively can yield critical outcomes in further developing your financial assessment. Consider factors, for example, loan costs, extraordinary equilibriums, and the effect of every obligation on your by and large monetary wellbeing. By zeroing in your endeavors on exorbitant interest obligations or those with the best potential to help your FICO rating, you can speed up your excursion toward obligation opportunity and monetary autonomy.

Fundamentally, taking care of obligation decisively is tied in with assuming command over your monetary predetermination and graphing a course toward a more brilliant monetary future. By investigating different obligation reimbursement strategies and focusing on obligations for greatest effect, you can make ready for a more grounded FICO rating and open a universe of monetary potential outcomes.

Using Credit Astutely

Becoming the best at utilizing credit shrewdly is a urgent move toward the mission to further develop your FICO rating and secure a strong monetary establishment. While credit can be an important instrument for accomplishing monetary objectives, it should be used with care and judiciousness to stay away from entanglements that can crash your credit process.

Offer Tips for Mindful Visa and Advance Use: Mastercards and credits are normal types of credit that numerous people use in their monetary lives. In any case, utilizing them dependably is critical to building a positive financial record and keeping major areas of strength for a score. Offer useful ways to oversee Mastercards and credits, like making ideal installments, keeping adjusts low, and staying away from pointless obligation collection. By sticking to these standards, people can show mindful credit the board and support their financial soundness over the long run.

Underline the Significance of Keeping up with Low Credit Use: Credit use, or the proportion of Visa adjusts as far as possible, assumes a huge part in deciding your FICO rating. High credit use can flag monetary trouble to loan specialists and adversely influence your FICO rating. Subsequently, it's significant to keep charge card adjusts low comparative with your credit limits. Urge people to take a stab at a credit usage proportion of 30% or lower, as this exhibits dependable credit the board and can add to a higher FICO rating.

Basically, using credit shrewdly is tied in with finding some kind of harmony between utilizing credit to accomplish monetary objectives and keeping up with restrained monetary propensities. By following tips for capable Mastercard and advance use and focusing on low credit use, people can explore the universe of credit with certainty and set before themselves a way toward further developed reliability and monetary achievement.

Tending to Negative Things on Your Credit Report

Facing negative things on your credit report head-on is an essential move toward the excursion toward further developing your FICO rating. While mishaps like assortments, late installments, and insolvencies can raise some serious questions about your financial record, they are not outlandish snags. With key activity and constancy, it's feasible to address and relieve the effect of these negative things on your FICO assessment.

Examine Procedures for Taking care of Assortments, Late Installments, and Liquidations: Assortments, late installments, and insolvencies are normal negative things that can altogether influence your financial assessment. Notwithstanding, there are procedures for tending to every one of these difficulties.

For assortments, consider arranging a repayment or installment plan with the bank to determine the obligation and possibly eliminate the assortment account from your credit report. Late installments can frequently be relieved by laying out a predictable example of on-time installments proceeding and mentioning generosity changes from lenders. Liquidations, while more extreme, can ultimately be eliminated from your credit report through time and tireless credit the board.

Give Moves toward Questioning Mistakes and Arranging Settlements: Errors on your credit report can unreasonably discolor your record and lower your financial assessment. Accordingly, it's fundamental to consistently survey your credit report for mistakes and errors and do whatever it takes to debate them with the credit departments. Furthermore, assuming you're confronting assortments or other negative things, consider arranging repayments with lenders to determine the obligations and possibly further develop your credit standing.

Generally, tending to negative things on your credit report requires a proactive and key methodology. By understanding how to deal with assortments, late installments, and liquidations and doing whatever it takes to question mistakes and arrange settlements, people can assume command over their credit predetermination and work toward accomplishing a more grounded and stronger credit profile.

Building Positive Credit Propensities

Developing positive credit propensities is fundamental for long haul monetary achievement and further developing your FICO rating. While tending to negative things on your credit report is vital, fostering a strong groundwork of positive credit propensities is similarly — while possibly not more — significant. These propensities act as the bedrock of a solid credit profile and lay the foundation for accomplishing and keeping a heavenly FICO rating.

Offer Noteworthy Guidance for Laying out a Strong Monetary Everyday practice: Building positive acknowledge propensities begins for laying out a strong monetary daily schedule. This incorporates making a spending plan, following costs, and living inside your means. By understanding your monetary circumstance and laying out sensible objectives, you can settle on informed choices that help your drawn out monetary prosperity.

Feature the Meaning of Consistency and Discipline in Credit The executives: Consistency and discipline are key parts of effective credit the board. Making on-time installments, keeping Visa adjusts low, and staying away from pointless obligation collection require responsibility and self-restraint. By focusing on these propensities and integrating them into your day to day monetary daily schedule, you can show to moneylenders and banks your unwavering quality and reliability as a borrower.

Basically, building positive credit propensities is tied in with encouraging a mentality of monetary obligation and responsibility. By embracing standards of planning, living inside your means, and keeping up with trained credit the executives rehearses, people can show themselves a way toward long haul monetary achievement and accomplish their objectives with certainty and security.

Chapter 4:
Maximizing Your
Credit Potential

Upgrading Credit Usage

Opening the maximum capacity of your credit process includes excelling at upgrading credit use. Your credit usage proportion — how much credit you're utilizing contrasted with your all out accessible credit — is a basic figure deciding your FICO rating. Thusly, understanding how to work out some kind of harmony and hold this proportion in line is fundamental for amplifying your credit potential.

Finding the Ideal Equilibrium for Visa Adjusts: Charge card adjusts assume a critical part in your credit usage proportion. While it's fundamental to use credit capably, conveying high adjusts can antagonistically affect your FICO assessment. In this way, endeavor to find the ideal harmony between utilizing Visas for comfort and keeping adjusts low to keep a solid credit use proportion.

Systems for Keeping Credit Use Low: Keeping credit use low requires a mix of vital preparation and restrained monetary propensities. Consider methodologies like taking care of balances in full every month, fanning out buys across different cards, and mentioning credit limit increments to diminish your use proportion. By carrying out these strategies, you can really deal with your credit usage and advance your credit potential.

Fundamentally, upgrading credit use is tied in with outfitting the force of credit mindfully to accomplish your monetary objectives while protecting your financial assessment. By understanding the significance of keeping a sound credit usage proportion and executing methodologies to keep adjusts low, you can open the maximum capacity of your credit and prepare for long haul monetary achievement.

Haggling with Leasers

Exploring the domain of credit includes dealing with your own monetary commitments as well as drawing in with leasers to improve your credit potential. Haggling with leasers can be an integral asset in your stockpile for further developing your credit standing and getting better terms on existing credit accounts.

Procedures for Bringing down Financing costs and Charges: Exorbitant loan costs and expenses can essentially influence your capacity to oversee obligation and keep a sound credit profile. Notwithstanding, numerous leasers will arrange lower rates and charges, particularly in the event that you have a past filled with capable credit the executives. Methods, for example, obligingly mentioning a rate decrease, refering to cutthroat offers, or utilizing dependability as a long-lasting client can frequently yield positive outcomes.

Ways to arrange Installment Plans or Settlements: On the off chance that you're battling to meet your monetary commitments, arranging installment plans or repayments with loan bosses can give alleviation and forestall further harm amazingly score. Be proactive in connecting with lenders to talk about your circumstance and propose doable reimbursement choices. Offering a singular amount settlement or consenting to an organized reimbursement plan may boost loan bosses to work with you and possibly moderate the effect on your credit.

Generally, haggling with lenders is tied in with supporting for you as well as your monetary prosperity. By utilizing methods to bring down loan costs and charges and arranging installment plans or repayments when fundamental, you can successfully deal with your obligation commitments and further develop your general credit standing.

Making arrangements for What's in store

Diagramming a course for long haul monetary achievement involves vital preparation and judicious administration of your credit assets. As you endeavor to boost your credit potential, it's fundamental to take on a ground breaking approach that lines up with your overall monetary objectives and yearnings.

Long haul Procedures for Keeping up with and Further developing FICO ratings: Keeping a heavenly FICO rating requires progressing persistence and scrupulousness. Foster long haul methodologies for overseeing acknowledge dependably, for example, reliably making on-time installments, keeping credit usage low, and consistently observing your credit report for mistakes. By carrying out these systems reliably over the long haul, you can defend your FICO assessment and position yourself for proceeded with monetary achievement.

Putting forth Monetary Objectives and Using Credit Admirably to Accomplish Them: Your credit process ought to be directed by clear and feasible monetary objectives. Whether you're meaning to purchase a home, begin a business, or resign serenely, having a guide set up can assist you with coming to informed conclusions about how to use credit to accomplish your targets. Use credit admirably to help your monetary objectives, whether through essential acquiring to support speculations or utilizing Mastercards to procure rewards that line up with your needs.

Fundamentally, anticipating what's to come includes adopting a proactive and all encompassing strategy to dealing with your credit and funds. By growing long haul systems for keeping up with and further developing your FICO ratings and adjusting your credit use to your more extensive monetary objectives, you can get yourself positioned for a future loaded up with monetary solidness, security, and achievement.

Chapter 5

Chapter 5: Advanced Credit Strategies

Figuring out Credit Requests

Diving into cutting edge credit systems requires a far reaching comprehension of credit requests — a basic part of credit the executives that can essentially influence your FICO rating and monetary standing. Whether you're applying for another Mastercard, looking for an advance, or even checking your own credit report, every request makes an imprint on your record of loan repayment, impacting your reliability in different ways.

What Requests Mean for Your Score and Overseeing Them Really: Perceiving the differentiation between two kinds of requests: hard requests and delicate inquiries is fundamental. Hard requests, started by moneylenders when you apply for credit, can marginally bring down your FICO rating and stay on your credit report for as long as two years. Delicate requests, then again, are requests made for educational purposes and don't influence your FICO assessment. Understanding the effect of these requests and overseeing them successfully is significant for keeping a sound credit profile.

Separating Among Hard and Delicate Requests: Having the option to separate among hard and delicate requests is vital to dealing with your credit actually. While hard requests might adversely affect your financial assessment, delicate requests make no difference and are regularly produced when you actually look at your own credit or when potential leasers pre-support you for offers. By understanding the nature and ramifications of each sort of request, you can arrive at informed conclusions about when and how to apply for credit, limiting pointless hits shockingly score.

Generally, dominating the subtleties of credit requests enables you to explore the acknowledge scene for certainty and accuracy. By understanding what requests mean for your FICO assessment and recognizing hard and delicate requests, you can decisively deal with your credit applications and shield your reliability for long haul monetary achievement.

Overseeing Credit During Life Changes

Life is loaded up with changes, both arranged and surprising, that can influence your credit and monetary prosperity. Whether you're beginning a new position, getting hitched, purchasing a home, or confronting a monetary misfortune, dealing with your credit really during these life altering events is significant for keeping areas of strength for an establishment.

Exploring Credit Changes During Significant Life altering Situations: Significant life altering situations like marriage, separate, or the introduction of a kid can have critical monetary ramifications, including changes surprisingly profile. It's fundamental to expect these progressions and proactively deal with your credit to alleviate any adverse consequences. For instance, refreshing your conjugal status with loan bosses or laying out discrete credit accounts after a separation can assist with keeping up with individual records.

Procedures for Limiting Adverse consequences On layaway: During seasons of change, it's critical to focus on monetary strength and limit activities that could adversely influence your credit. This might incorporate staying away from new credit applications, continuing existing credit accounts on favorable terms, and speaking with leasers assuming you expect trouble meeting installment commitments. By remaining proactive and informed, you can explore life changes with negligible disturbance surprisingly profile.

Generally, overseeing credit during life changes requires a proactive and versatile methodology. By expecting monetary changes, remaining informed about your credit status, and making key moves to safeguard your credit, you can explore life's advances with certainty and keep a strong monetary starting point for what's in store.

Safeguarding Your Credit Personality

Shielding your credit personality is fundamental in the present computerized age, where the gamble of misrepresentation and wholesale fraud poses a potential threat. Your credit data contains delicate information that, whenever split the difference, can unleash devastation on your monetary prosperity. Subsequently, going to proactive lengths to safeguard your credit personality is fundamental for keeping up with monetary security and true serenity.

Protecting Against Misrepresentation and Wholesale fraud: Character cheats are continually contriving better approaches to take advantage of weaknesses and take individual data for monetary benefit. Safeguard yourself by defending delicate records, destroying budget reports before removal, and being mindful while sharing individual data on the web or via telephone. Moreover, consider signing up for data fraud insurance administrations and observing your credit consistently for indications of dubious movement.

Ventures for Checking and Getting Your Credit Data: Ordinary observing of your credit report is a pivotal part of credit personality security. Exploit free credit reports from the significant credit agencies and audit them for errors or unapproved accounts. Consider setting a misrepresentation caution or credit freeze on your credit record to forestall unapproved access. By remaining careful and proactive, you can distinguish and address possible dangers surprisingly character before they grow into major monetary issues.

Generally, safeguarding your credit character requires a proactive and diverse methodology. By executing safety efforts to protect delicate data, checking your credit routinely for indications of unapproved action, and making a quick move to resolve any issues that emerge, you can strengthen your guards against extortion and fraud and save your monetary prosperity.

Accomplishing Monetary Objectives through Credit Dominance

Dominating the complexities of credit not just engages you to explore the monetary scene with certainty yet additionally fills in as an integral asset for accomplishing your drawn out monetary objectives. As you endeavor to boost your credit potential, it's vital for influence your incredible credit remaining to open doors and impel yourself toward monetary development and strength.

Utilizing Brilliant Credit to Open doors: A solid credit profile opens ways to a heap of chances, from getting positive advance terms to meeting all requirements for premium Mastercards with worthwhile prizes. Exploit your fantastic credit remaining to get to credit items and administrations that line up with your monetary objectives, whether it's getting a home loan for your fantasy home, funding an undertaking, or venturing to the far corners of the planet with remunerations focuses.

Systems for Involving Credit as a Device for Monetary Development and Steadiness: Credit, when utilized shrewdly, can be an impetus for monetary development and strength. Consider key ways of utilizing credit to accomplish your monetary targets, for example, putting resources into resources that value after some time, subsidizing training or expert improvement open doors, or uniting exorbitant interest obligation to bring down your general acquiring costs. By involving credit as a device to create financial wellbeing and secure your monetary future, you can change your fantasies into the real world and make a tradition of monetary achievement.

Generally, accomplishing monetary objectives through credit dominance requires vision, discipline, and vital preparation. By saddling the force of superb credit to open doors and involving credit as a device for monetary development and solidness, you can diagram a course toward a more splendid and more prosperous future for you as well as your friends and family.

Conclusion: Mastering Your Credit Journey

Pondering Your Advancement

As you arrive at the finish of your credit process, it's vital for pause for a minute to consider the headway you've made and the achievements you've accomplished en route. Consider how far you've come from the outset of your excursion, the information you've acquired, and the abilities you've created in dealing with your credit really.

Considering the Information and Abilities Acquired: Ponder the significant experiences you've procured about credit the executives, from understanding FICO ratings and reports to carrying out techniques for improving and keeping up with your financial soundness. Consider how this freshly discovered information has enabled you to settle on additional educated monetary choices and explore the intricacies of the acknowledge scene for certainty.

Observing Achievements and Achievements: Credit authority is quite difficult, and each achievement you've reached merits acknowledgment and festivity. Whether you've effectively taken care of obligation, accomplished a higher FICO rating, or protected a credit with good terms, invest heavily in your achievements and recognize the difficult work and commitment that have carried you to this point.

Fundamentally, considering your advancement permits you to recognize how far you've come on your credit process and gives inspiration to push ahead. By perceiving your accomplishments and the development you've encountered, you can reaffirm your obligation to dominating your credit and building a more splendid monetary future for you as well as your friends and family.

Focusing on Continuous Learning and Improvement

As you finish up your credit process, it's vital to perceive that dominating credit isn't an objective but instead a ceaseless course of learning and improvement. The monetary scene is continually developing, and remaining educated and versatile is critical to keeping up with your monetary wellbeing and accomplishing your drawn out objectives.

Perceiving That Dominating Credit is a Continuous Interaction: Credit the executives is dynamic, with new guidelines, innovations, and monetary items constantly arising. Recognize that your excursion toward dominating credit is continuous and that there will constantly be amazing open doors for development and improvement. Embrace the attitude of long lasting learning and stay open to gaining new information and abilities to remain ahead in the always impacting monetary world.

Resolving to Proceeded with Schooling and Development: Promise to focus on continuous training and development in your monetary excursion. Remain refreshed on changes in credit regulations and guidelines, investigate new methodologies for streamlining your credit potential, and search out assets like books, courses, and workshops to develop how you might interpret credit the executives standards. By putting resources into your monetary instruction, you enable yourself to adjust to changing conditions and explore future difficulties with certainty.

Fundamentally, focusing on continuous learning and improvement is fundamental for keeping up with dominance over your credit and guaranteeing long haul monetary achievement.

By perceiving that credit the executives is a consistent excursion and embracing potential open doors for development and training, you can situate yourself to flourish in any monetary climate and accomplish your objectives with clearness and flexibility.

Engaging Yourself Through Monetary Proficiency

At the center of dominating your credit process lies the amazing asset of monetary proficiency. Monetary education enables you to come to informed conclusions about your funds, including overseeing credit actually, planning shrewdly, and making arrangements for what's in store. As you close your credit process, it's fundamental to perceive the job that monetary proficiency plays in molding your monetary prosperity and focus on continuous endeavors to improve your insight and understanding.

Embracing the Force of Monetary Education to Pursue Informed Choices: Monetary proficiency outfits you with the information and abilities expected to certainly explore the intricacies of the monetary world. From understanding the variables that impact your FICO assessment to assessing credit terms and speculation open doors, monetary proficiency enables you to pursue sound monetary choices that line up with your objectives and values.

Understanding That Information is Critical to Accomplishing Monetary Freedom and Security: Information is an amazing asset that can prepare to monetary autonomy and security. By putting resources into your monetary schooling and constantly extending how you might interpret credit and individual accounting, you oversee your monetary fate and diminish the gamble of succumbing to monetary entanglements and tricks. Perceive that the more you are familiar credit and cash the board, the better prepared you'll be to fabricate areas of strength for an establishment for you as well as your loved ones.

Basically, enabling yourself through monetary proficiency is fundamental for dominating your credit process and making enduring monetary progress. By embracing the force of information and focusing on continuous learning and improvement, you can assume command over your monetary future and make an existence of monetary overflow and security.

Assuming Command over Your Monetary Future

As you arrive at the finish of your credit process, now is the ideal time to take responsibility for monetary future and set up as a regular occurrence the techniques and standards you've advanced en route. Assuming command over your monetary fate includes executing the illustrations you've gained, defining clear objectives, and pursuing purposeful decisions that line up with your vision for what's in store.

Engaging Yourself to Assume Command over Your Monetary Fate: Perceive that you have the ability to shape your monetary future through your activities and choices. By taking responsibility for monetary circumstance and declining to be aloof observers to your monetary predetermination, you enable yourself to make the existence you want. Embrace the outlook of monetary strengthening and find proactive ways to construct a protected and prosperous future for you as well as your friends and family.

Focusing on Executing Techniques Figured out how to Fabricate a More splendid Monetary Future: Set up as a regular occurrence the information and abilities you've acquired all through your credit process to lay the foundation for a more splendid monetary future. Whether it's taking care of obligation, constructing a rainy day account, or contributing as long as possible, focus on executing the procedures and standards you've figured out how to accomplish your monetary objectives. Remain restrained, keep on track, and remain focused on your monetary achievement.

Basically, assuming command over your monetary future is tied in with holding onto the reins of your monetary fate and controlling it toward your fantasies. By enabling yourself to pursue informed choices, putting forth clear objectives, and making deliberate moves, you can make an existence of monetary overflow, security, and satisfaction.